BEGINNING BOOGIE & RAGS FOR PIANO

Boston Music Company

Published by
Boston Music Company

Exclusive Distributors:

Hal Leonard,
7777 West Bluemound Road,
Milwaukee, WI 53213
Email: info@halleonard.com

Hal Leonard Europe Limited,
42 Wigmore Street Maryleborne,
London, W1U 2 RY
Email: info@halleonardeurope.com

Hal Leonard Australia Pty. Ltd.
4 Lentara Court Cheltenham,
Victoria, 9132 Australia
Email: info@halleonard.com.au

Order No. BM11858
ISBN 1-84609-468-2

This book C Copyright 2006
Boston Music Company

Series Editor David Harrison.
Cover designed by Michael Bell Design.
Cover picture from 1926, American ragtime pianist Eubie Blake and singer Noble Sissle,
courtesy of Frank Driggs Collection / Contributor / Getty Images.

Printed in EU.

www.halleonard.com

Basic Boogie

Frank Metis

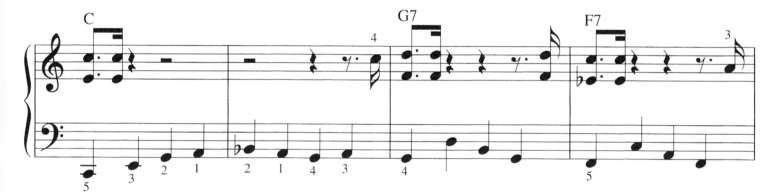

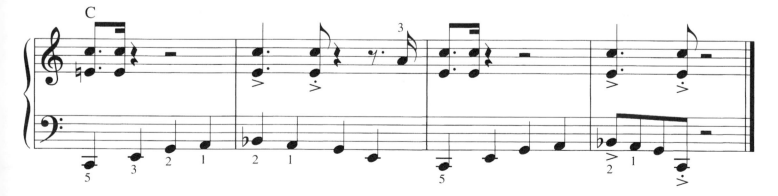

Living A Ragtime Life

Roberts & Jefferson

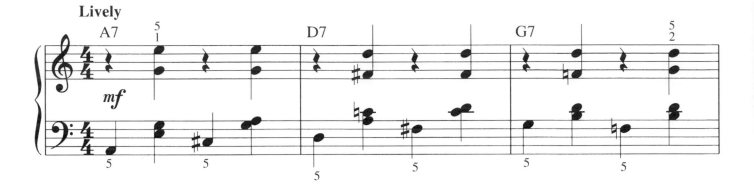

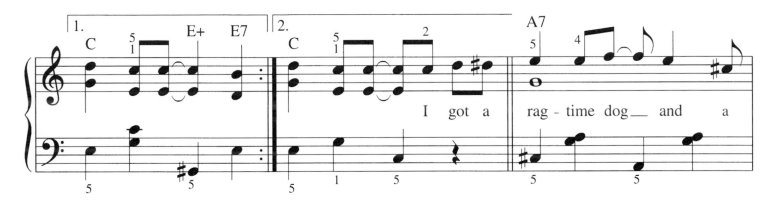

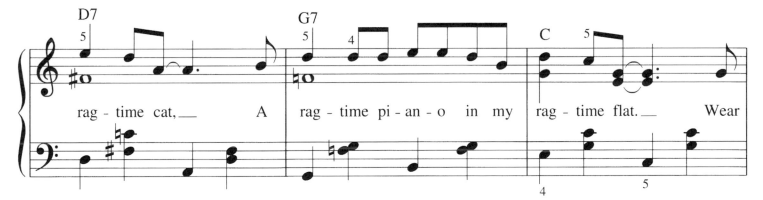

"Rag - time News."___ Got rag - time hab-its and I talk that way. _ I

sleep in rag-time and I rag all day. _ Got rag - time trou-bles with my

rag - time wife, _ I'm cer-tain-ly liv-ing a rag - time life.

The Battle Of Jericho

Traditional

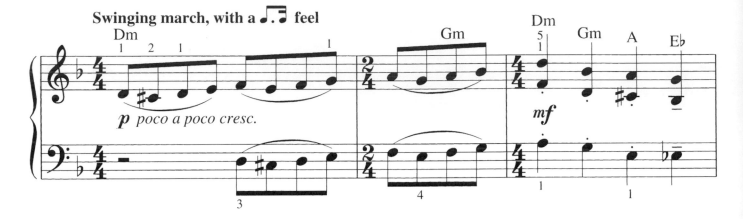

Black And White Rag

George Botsford

Moderately lively

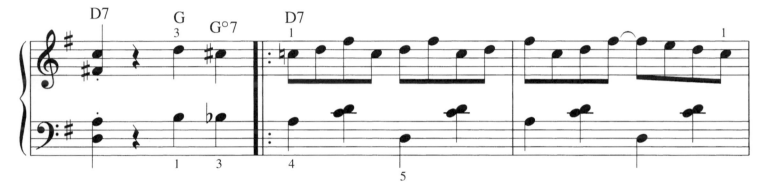

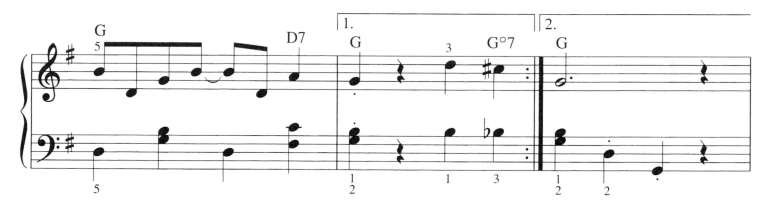

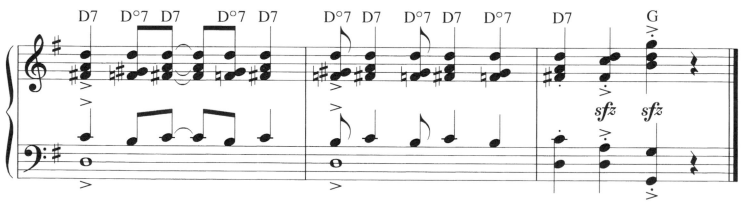

9

Bill Bailey, Won't You Please Come Home?

Words & Music by Hughie Cannon

won't you come home?" She cried the

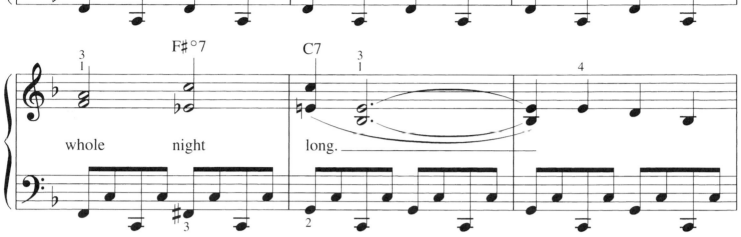

whole night long. "I'll do the dish – es, hon – ey,

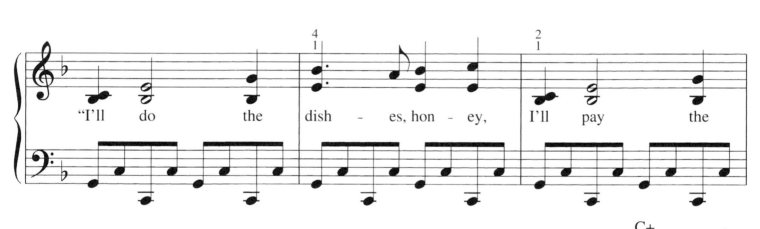

I'll pay the

rent. I know I done you

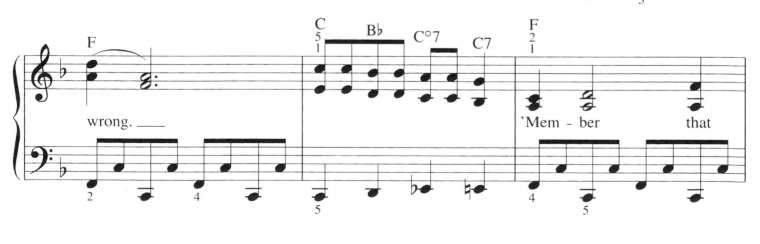

wrong. 'Mem – ber that

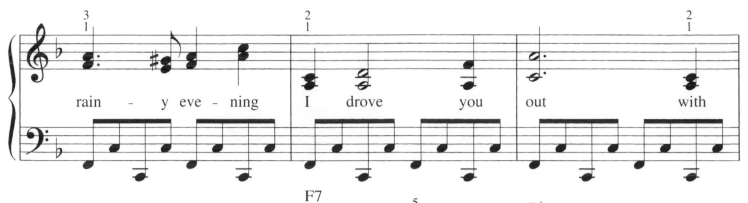

rain - y eve - ning I drove you out with

noth - ing but a fine - tooth comb?

I know I'm to blame, Well,

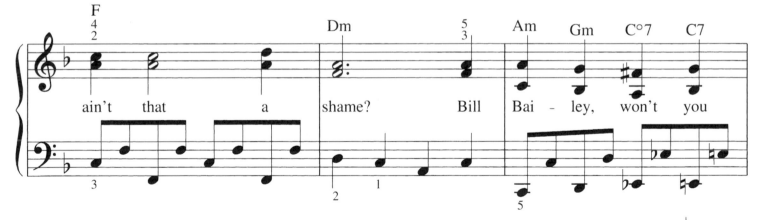

ain't that a shame? Bill Bai - ley, won't you

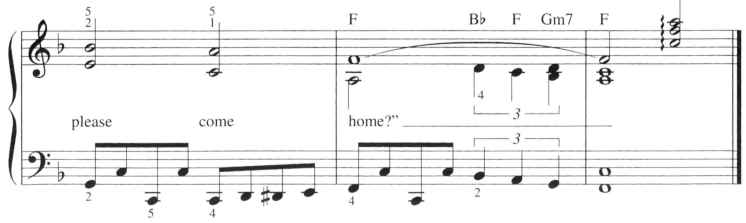

please come home?"

Weeping Willow

Scott Joplin

Moderately slow

Yankee Doodle

Traditional

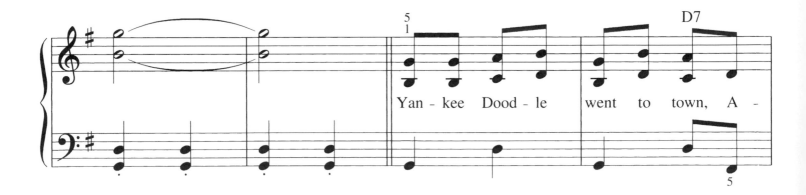

Yan - kee Dood - le went to town, A -

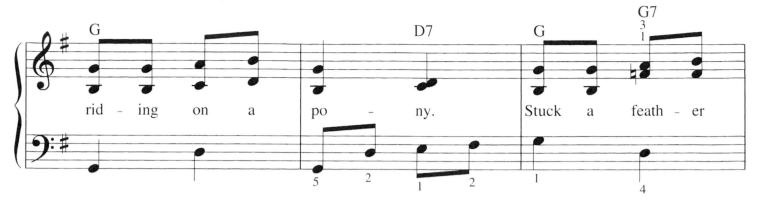

 rid – ing on a po – ny. Stuck a feath – er

in his hat and called it mac – a – ro – ni.

Chorus

Yan – kee Dood – le keep it up, Yan – kee Dood – le

dan – dy. Mind the mu – sic and the step and

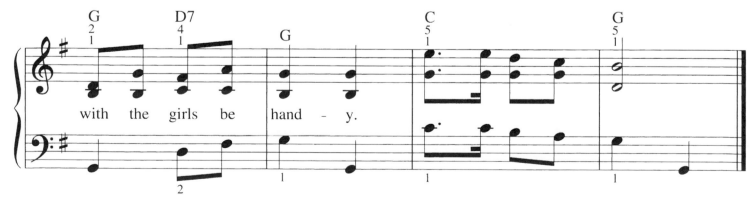

with the girls be hand – y.

15

The Entertainer

Scott Joplin

Not too fast

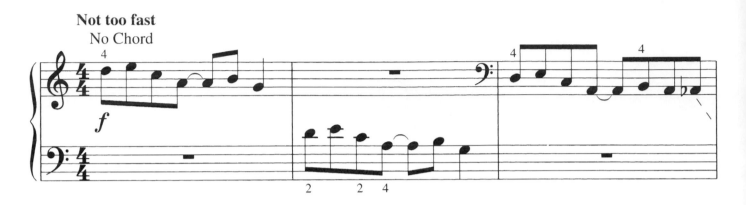

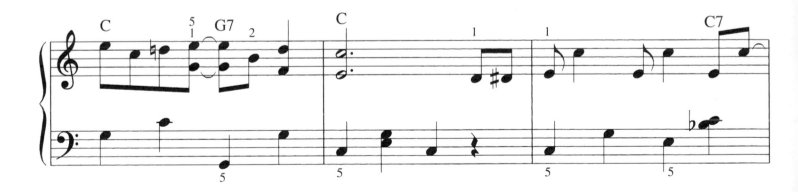

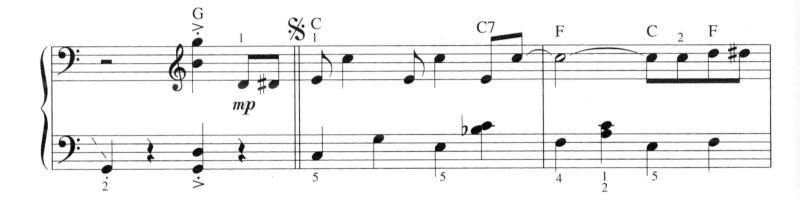

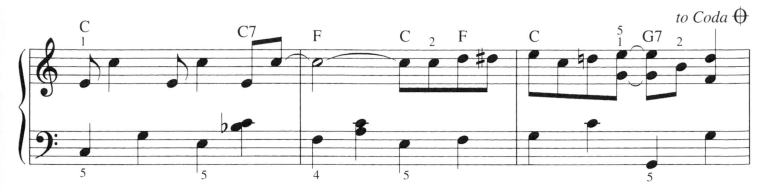

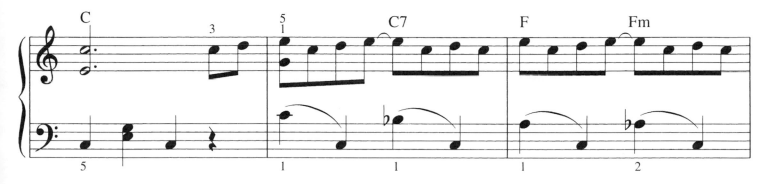

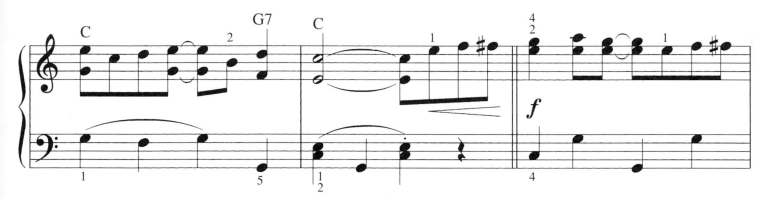

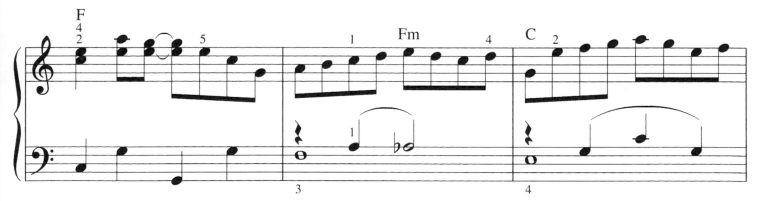

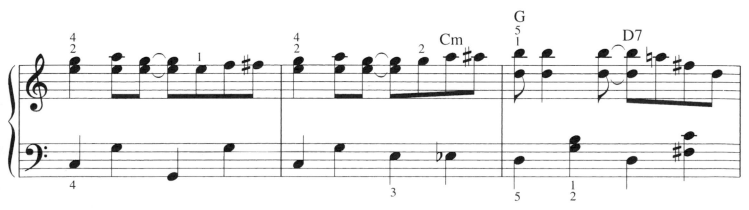

17

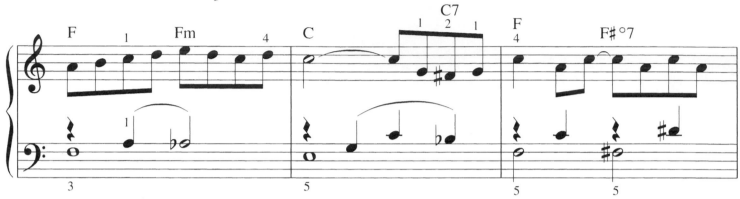

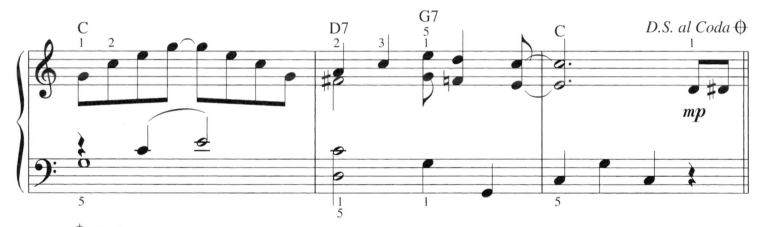

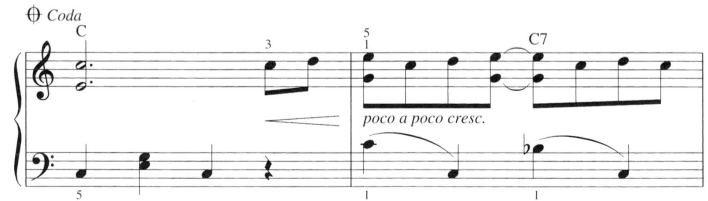

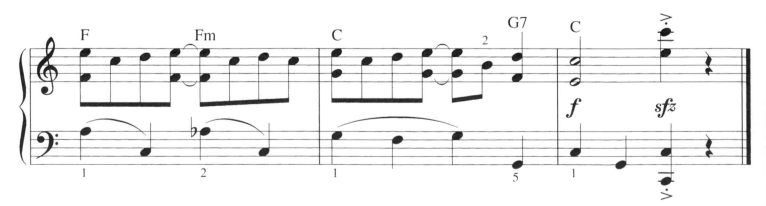

Prayer Parade

Frank Metis

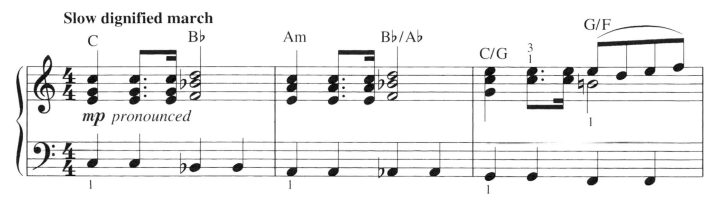

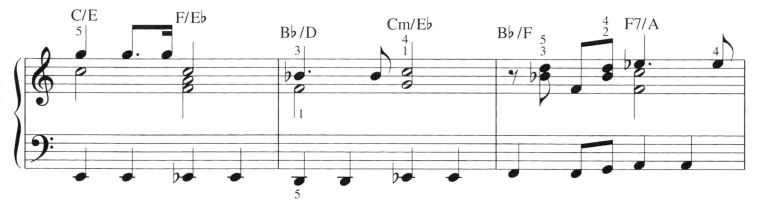

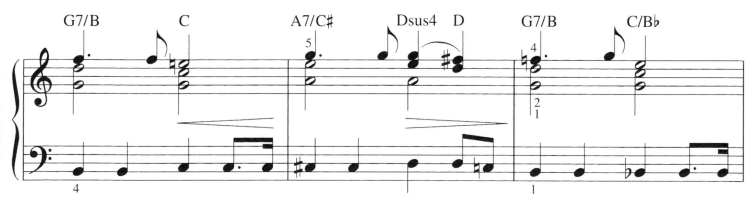

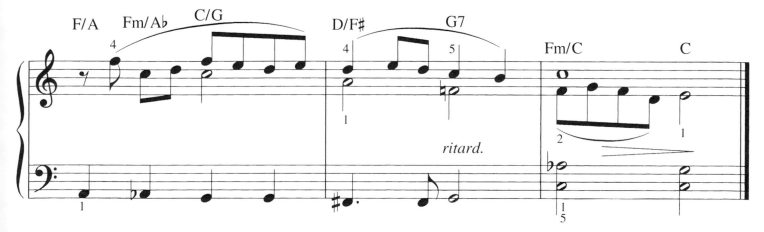

Broadway Parade

Frank Metis

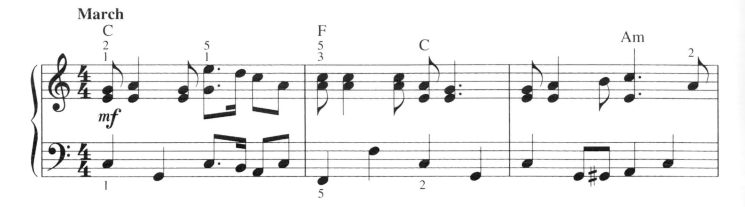

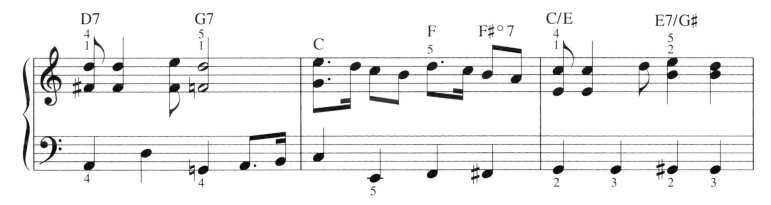

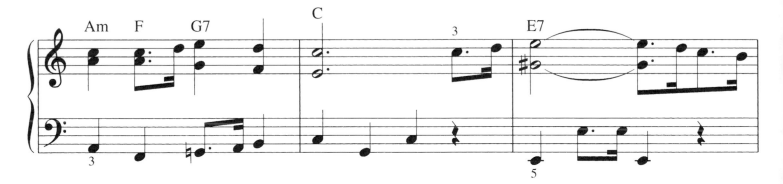

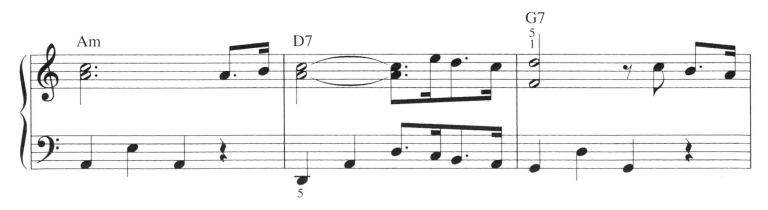

poco a poco cresc.

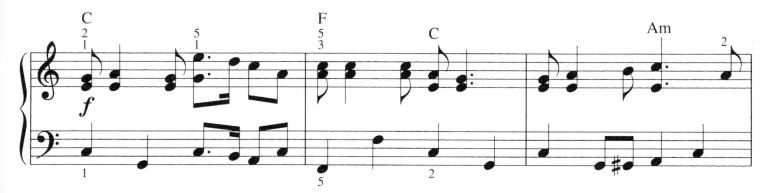

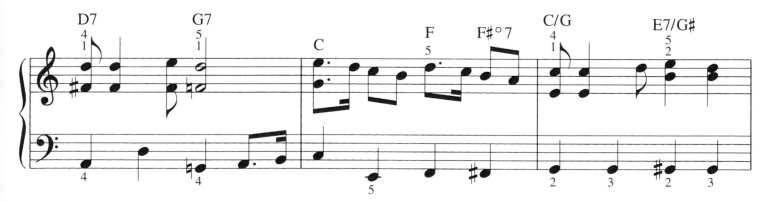

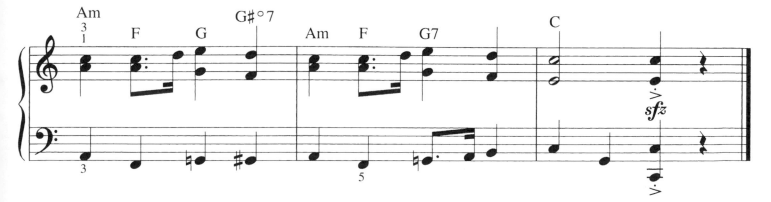

Ballin' The Jack Boogie

Words by James Henry Burris
Music by Chris Smith

Moderately, with a steady beat

First you put your two knees close up tight, — Then you sway 'em to the left, then you sway 'em to the right, Step a - round the floor kind of nice and light, — Then you

Palm Leaf Rag

Scott Joplin

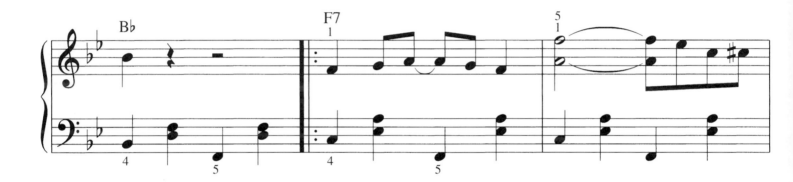

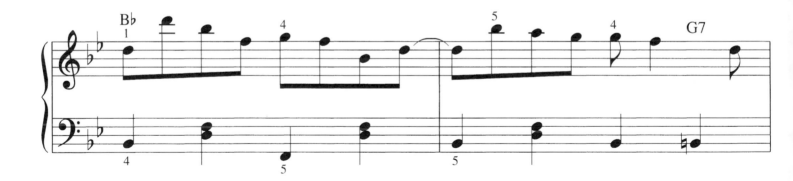

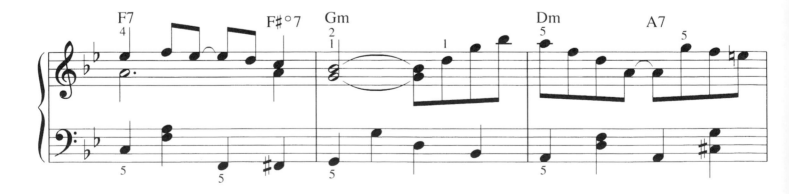

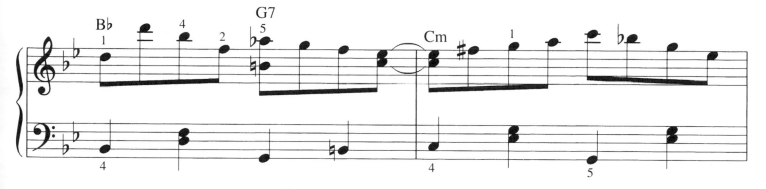

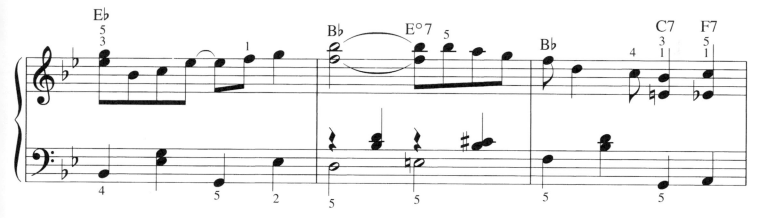

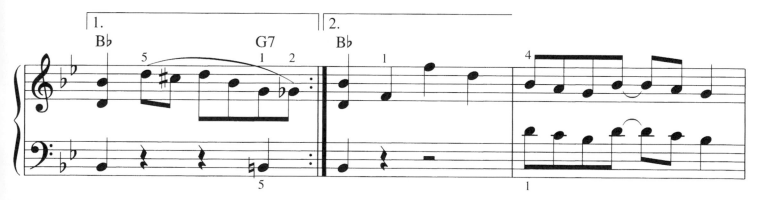

25

Ragtime Cowboy Joe

Words & Music by Lewis F. Muir,
Grant Clark & Maurice Abrahams

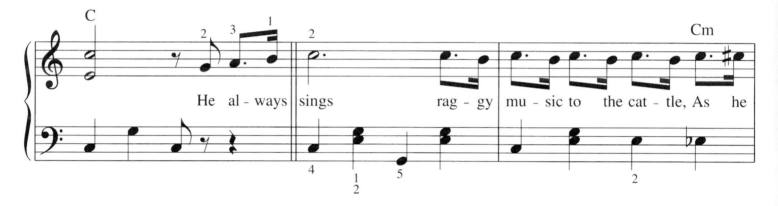

He al-ways sings rag-gy mu-sic to the cat-tle, As he

swings back and for-ward in the sad-dle, On a horse that is

syn-co-pat-ed gait-ed, And there's such a fun-ny me-ter, To the

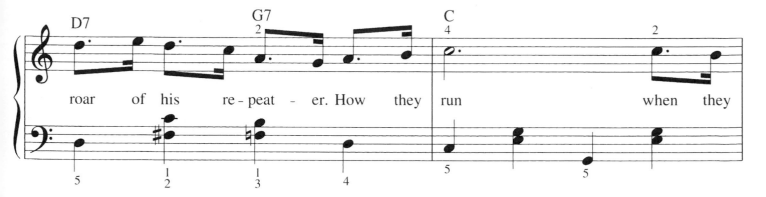

roar of his re - peat - er. How they run when they

hear that fel - low's gun, Be-cause the west - ern folks all

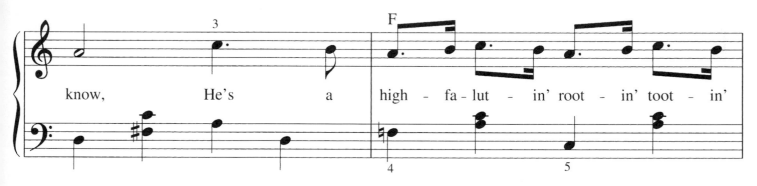

know, He's a high - fa - lut - in' root - in' toot - in'

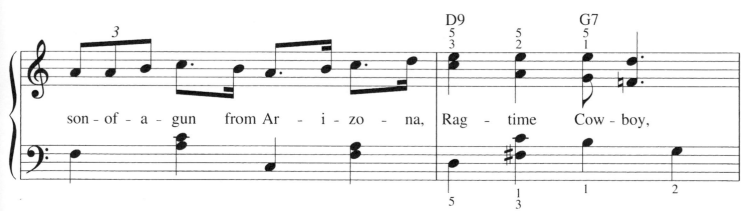

son - of - a - gun from Ar - i - zo - na, Rag - time Cow - boy,

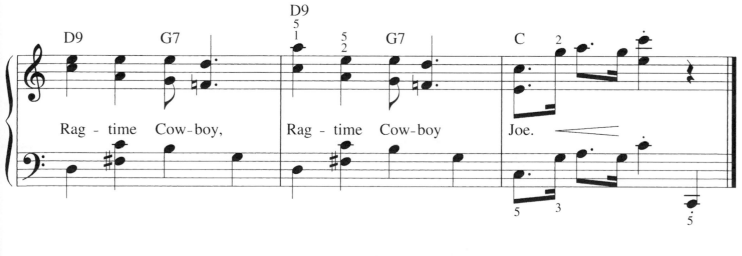

Rag - time Cow-boy, Rag - time Cow-boy Joe.

Changing Times

Frank Metis

Boogie waltz, moderately

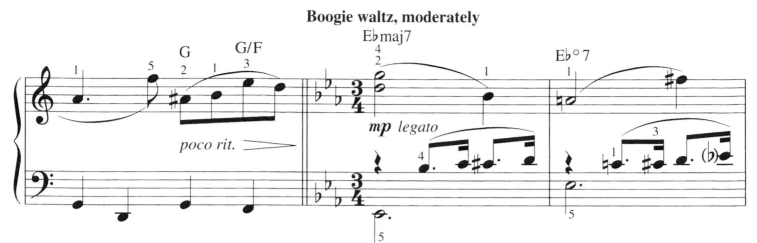

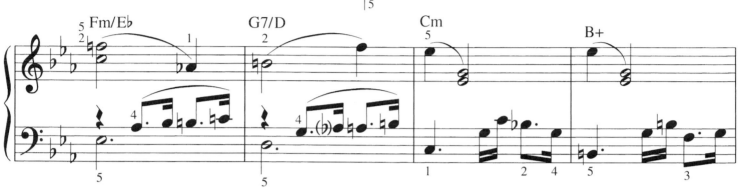

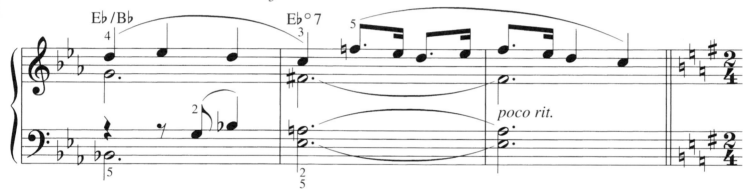

Ragtime, moderately bright

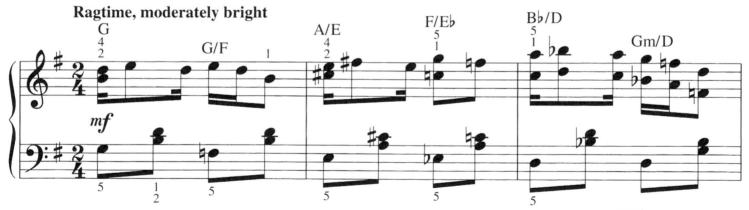

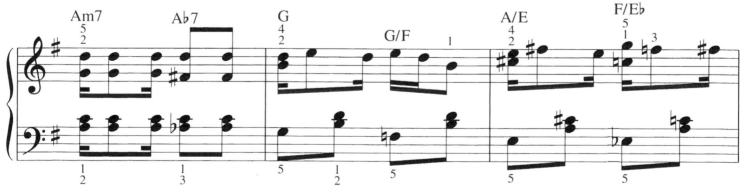

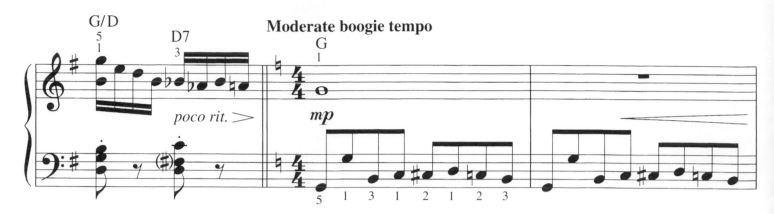

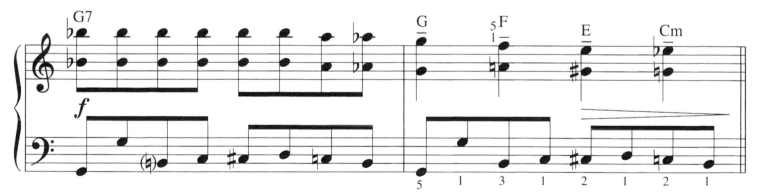

Moderate march (as before)

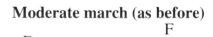

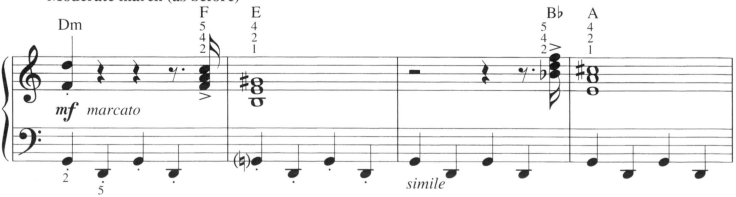

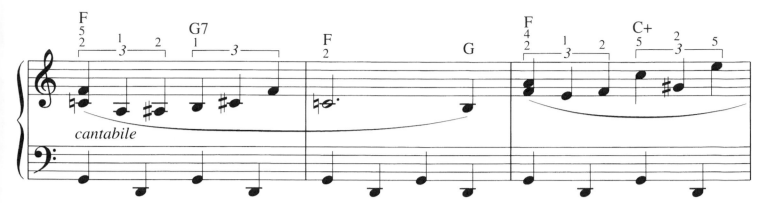

Boogie waltz (as before)

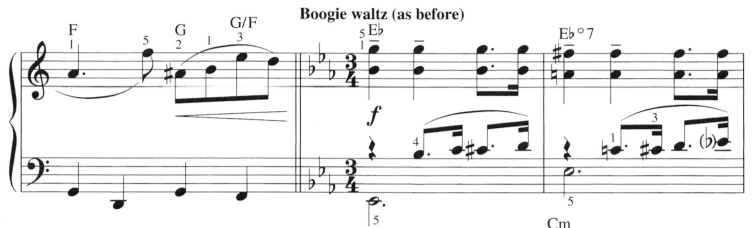

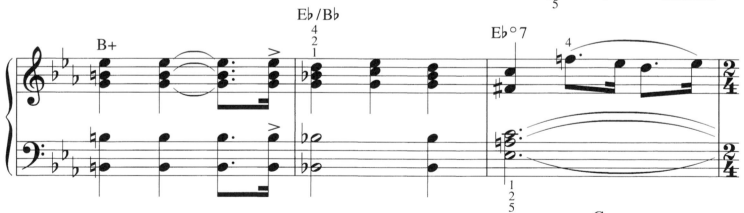